Basic Supplies:

- needle nose pliers or tweezers—to tighten knots and attach jump rings
- large split ring
- scissors

About the Cord:

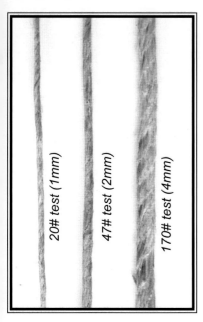

20# test (1mm)   47# test (2mm)   170# test (4mm)

Hemp is preferred to other fiber cords for jewelry because it knots easily and holds knots well without requiring glue. It is also smooth enough to be comfortable next to the skin. Jute cord is similar in appearance but too scratchy to wear. Hemp comes in a variety of sizes and finishes, from thread-weight to heavy rope. Two sizes are commonly used for making knotted and braided jewelry:

    20# (about 1 millimeter)

    45–50# (about 2mm)

Heavier cords, from 100# to 200#, are occasionally sold for jewelry. They are usually less regular in thickness than the lighter weights and produce a more massive, rustic look best for very simple projects such as flat braided belts. The projects in this book use 1mm or 2mm hemp cord, although many could be made in a heavier weight.

The natural color of hemp is a medium tan. Jewelry-weight hemp dyed to various bright colors is available, but can be difficult to find. Waxed cotton or linen twine can be substituted for 1mm hemp if colored jewelry is desired. DO NOT use waxed nylon or polyester, as they fray too easily and knots will slip.

About Beads:

Hemp works well with a variety of bead types. Wood and ceramic beads emphasize its natural character. The dull patina of unlacquered brass complements the color. The matte look of polymer clay beads is ideal—and they are available in many intricate designs. Plastic, glass, bright lacquered or antiqued metallic beads, even iridescent and faceted crystal beads contrast with the dull tan to produce widely differing effects. Be sure the beads you use have large enough holes—many patterns require two or more strands of hemp to go through each bead, and too-small or barely-big-enough holes are a real pain to work with. When you go bead shopping, carry a strand of each size cord you plan to use to try with the beads. Bead sizes are usually given in millimeters. Use the chart to estimate how big your beads need to be.

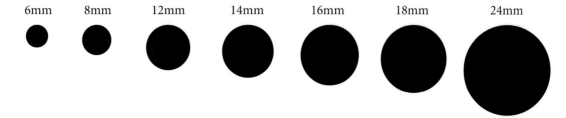

6mm   8mm   12mm   14mm   16mm   18mm   24mm

Produced by **HOT OFF THE PRESS, INC.**, for distribution exclusively by Leisure Arts, Inc., 5701 Ranch Drive, Little Rock, Arkansas 72223-9633, **leisurearts.com**. Projects by Marty Hite and Katie Hacker.

We have made every effort to ensure that these instructions are accurate and complete. We cannot, however, be responsible for human error, typographical mistakes, or variations in individual work.

overhand knots

BASIC KNOTS:

An **overhand** knot is tied in a single strand, or – more often – in a group of strands held together

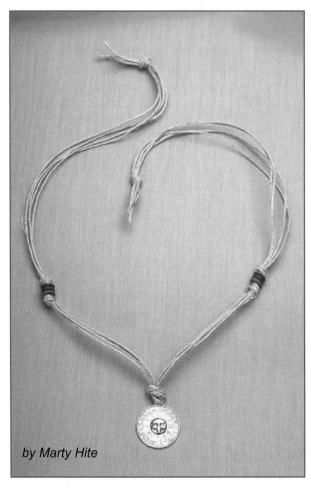

by Marty Hite

Super-Simple Zodiac Necklace

four 30" lengths of 1mm hemp cord
one 1" wide antique pewter zodiac charm

two 9x7mm etched terra cotta tube beads
one 8mm silver jump ring
basic supplies (see page 1)

1 Attach the charm to the jump ring (see p. 32). Insert all four strands through the jump ring and center the charm on the strands. Tie an overhand knot above the charm.

2 Separate the strands into two groups of four. **On each group:** Tie an overhand knot 3½" from the first knot. Slide a terra cotta bead over all the strands up to the knot. Tie another overhand knot. Tie another knot 1" from the end of the strands. **To wear:** Tie the ends together behind your neck. **Optional:** Make a clasp by knotting one end again ½" from the first knot to form a loop. Slip the knot on the other end through the loop.

Poem Candleholder

Wrap one long strand around the vase twice, then tie in an overhand knot. Insert through a yellow bead, then overhand knot. Repeat with a turquoise bead, blue bead and silver bead. Finish with an overhand knot and trim the ends to ¼".

LAUGH with the clouds
DANCE with the trees
SING with the stars
SMILE at the fish
····Breathe Deeply····

Be Amazed!

····by K. Hacker····

by Katie Hacker

Charm Necklace

six 24" lengths of 1mm hemp cord
glass crow beads or transparent plastic
   pony beads: 2 blue, 2 green, 2 red, 1
   amber
1"x1½" antique silver charm
one 8mm silver jump ring
optional: masking tape
basic supplies (see page 1)

by Marty Hite

1 Before beginning, attach the jump ring to the eye of the charm (see page 32). Hold all the strands together and tie an overhand knot in the end. Thread all the strands through the amber bead and slide the bead up to the knot. Separate the strands into three groups of two. Braid a double 3-strand braid (see below) for 7".

2 Tie the outer strand pairs in a half knot around the center pair. String a blue, a green and a red bead over the center strands and tie a half knot as before.

3 Braid for ¾" and tie a half knot as before. Insert the bottom four strands through the jump ring and finish a square knot. Continue, reversing the sequence of knots, braid and beads for the second half of the necklace.

4 Tie a half square knot as before. Leave a ½" gap, then tie an overhand knot. To clasp, slip the beginning knot and bead through the end loop – it should be a tight fit.

3-STRAND BRAID:

(A) Bring the right strand over the center, then (B) bring the left strand over the center. Tighten the braid. Repeat to the desired length.

4-STRAND BRAID:

(A) Bring the left strand over the second, under the third and over the fourth strand. Tighten. (B) Bring the new left strand over the second, under the third and over the fourth. Repeat to the desired length.

DOUBLE BRAID:

Braid a 3- or 4-strand braid using two strands for each one shown in the first two photos. Be careful to keep the braid flat – it helps to secure a long braid every 1"-2" with masking tape. Remove the tape after the braiding is finished.

Yin/Yang World Bracelet

1mm hemp cord: two 18", two 36" strands
two ½" wide black & white "yin-yang" millefiori disk beads
one ½" wide green/turquoise "world" millefiori disk bead
basic supplies (see page 1)

by Marty Hite

1 Hold all the lengths together and tie an overhand knot close to one end. Braid a four-strand braid for 2", ending with the short strands in the center and the long strands outside. Use the outer strands to tie 2" of square knot sinnet over the inner strands.

2 Slide a yin-yang bead over the two center strands; push it up to the last knot. Bring the outside strands around the bead and tie one complete square knot over the center strands.

3 Repeat step 2 with the world bead, then with the second yin-yang bead. Tie a 2" square knot sinnet. Braid a four-strand braid for 2", then tie an overhand knot. Trim the hemp close to the knots on each end. **To wear:** Wrap the bracelet around your wrist or ankle and tie the braided ends in a square knot.

Tube Bead Bracelet

1mm hemp cord: two 18", two 36" strands
fourteen 8x6mm ceramic tube beads, assorted colors
basic supplies (see page 1)

by Marty Hite

1 Hold all four strands together and secure to a ring with an overhand knot. Braid a 4-strand braid for 2", ending with the short strands in the center and the long strands to the outside.

2 Tie a 2" square knot sinnet. Slide the first bead over the two center strands and push it close to the last knot. Bring the outside strands around the bead and tie one complete square knot over the center strands.

3 Repeat, adding beads and making square knots until all the beads are used. Tie a 2" square knot sinnet, then braid a 4-strand braid for 2". Remove from the ring and tighten the knots. Trim the ends 1" from the knots. **To wear:** Wrap the bracelet around your wrist or ankle and tie the braided ends in a square knot.

SQUARE KNOT SINNET:

A sinnet is a series of knots worked around unworked or "droned" strands. In the square knot sinnet, only the two outer strands are worked; there may be one, two (usually) or more drone strands.

1 Make a half knot, with the left strand passing in front of the drone strands and the right passing behind, so that the drone strands are enclosed in a loop.

2 Make another half knot with the right strand passing in front – this completes a square knot. Continue for the desired length.

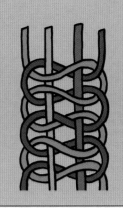

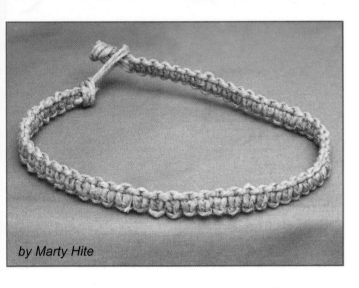

by Marty Hite

(*This makes a 15" choker. The length required may vary according to how tightly you knot as well as how long you want the choker.)

Square Knot Choker

2mm hemp cord: one *5-yard length, one 36" length
basic supplies (see page 1)

1 Hold the strands together with the short one centered on the long one. Fold them in half around a securing ring and tie an overhand knot 1" below the fold.

2 Tie a 13" (or your neck measurement plus 1") square knot sinnet. Leave a ½" gap and tie an overhand knot. Remove from the ring and tighten both knots. Trim the ends close to the knots. **To clasp:** Slip the end knot through the beginning loop.

Purple Center Bead Bracelet

1mm hemp cord: one 18", two 36" strands
one 15mm purple glass bicone bead with squared sides
two 5x8mm silver oval beads
basic supplies (see page 1)

1 Hold all the lengths together and tie an overhand knot close to one end. Braid a 3-strand braid for 1½", ending with the short strand in the center and the long strands outside. Tie a 4" square knot sinnet.

2 Slide a silver bead over the center strand and snug it up to the last knot. Bring the outside strands around the bead and tie two complete square knots over the center strand.

by Marty Hite

3 Repeat step 2 with the glass bead, then with the second silver bead. Tie a 4" square knot sinnet. Braid a 3-strand braid for 1½", then tie an overhand knot. Trim the hemp 1½" from the knots on each end. **To wear:** Wrap the bracelet around your wrist or ankle and tie the braided ends in a square knot.

by Katie Hacker
actual length 2"

Blue Bead Earrings

six 6" lengths of 20# test hemp
two 14mm round blue/gold glass beads
two gold ear wires
two 8mm round gold jump rings
basic supplies (see page 1)

For each earring: Hold three strands together, ends even, and fold ½" through the jump ring. Tie the outer strands in two square knots, securing the ½" ends; trim these ends below the last knot. Slide the bead on the drone strand. Tie the strands in an overhand knot, then trim the ends to ¼". Attach the jump ring (see page 32) to the ear wire.

Multi-Bead Bracelet

by Marty Hite
length 11"

20# test hemp cord: one 2-yard, two 12" lengths
22 assorted 6-8mm glass and metal beads
basic supplies (see page 1)

1 Hold the 12" strands together, ends even. Tie the center of the 2-yard length around them in a half knot 2" from the ends. Slip the knot into a ring to secure. Place the ends of the long strand on the outside and tie three square knots around the center strand.

2 String one bead over the drone strands and tie a square knot. Repeat to use all the beads, then tie three square knots. Tie an overhand knot and trim the ends to 2". Slip the bracelet off the ring. **To clasp:** Tie the ends in a square knot.

Flower Necklace

20# test hemp cord: one 2¼-yard, two 5¼-yard lengths
round wood beads: six 8mm, four 16mm
basic supplies (see page 1)

1 Fold the strands in half over a ring and tie an overhand knot 1" from the fold. Arrange the strands with the short strands in the center. Tie a 5½" long square knot sinnet.

2 Slide a 16mm bead onto the drone strands, then continue tying square knots for 1½". Slide a 16mm bead onto the drone strands and three 8mm beads onto each set of working strands to form the flower.

3 Square knot for 1½, then slide a 16mm bead onto the drone strands. Square knot for 5½", then slide a 16mm bead over all the strands. Tie an overhand knot and trim the ends to ½". Slip the necklace off the ring. **To clasp:** Place the end bead through the beginning loop.

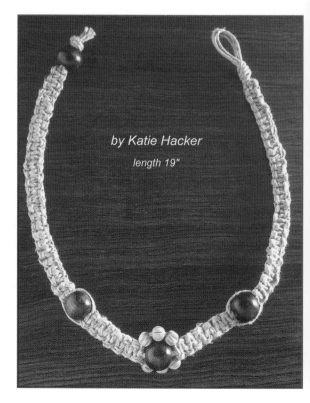

by Katie Hacker
length 19"

Beaded Key Ring

three 30" lengths of 1mm hemp cord
1" round split ring
6 transparent plastic pony beads: 4 turquoise, 2 cobalt

1 Fold each length in half and attach to the split ring with a lark's head knot (see drawing). Be sure the knots are loose enough to slide on the ring, or you won't be able to add and remove keys. Tie the outer strands in a square knot over the center four strands (there are four drone strands in this project).

2 Slide a turquoise bead over the center strands and up to the knot. Tie another square knot and add a cobalt bead, then another square knot and a turquoise bead.

by Marty Hite

3 Tie two complete square knots, then tie a half-knot sinnet for ½", or one complete turn of the spiral. Tie two more complete square knots, then repeat step 2. Tie all the strands in an overhand knot and trim the ends to 2" long.

Flower Necklace

1mm hemp cord: one 60", one 6-yard length
four 8mm brass bicone spacer beads
one 1¼" long gold leaf charm
one 10mm natural wooden bead
basic supplies (see page 1)

1 Center the short strand on the long one, fold in half over a ring and tie an overhand knot ¾" below the ring. Arrange the strands so the two short ends are in the center.

2 Tie a 1½" square knot sinnet. Tie a 1½" half knot sinnet (or four complete spirals). The last knot should lie in the same plane as the square knot sinnet.

3 Repeat step 2 twice more. String a brass bead over the two center strands and tie two more square knots. String another brass bead; tie two square knots. Slip the eye of the charm over one side strand and tie two more square knots.

4 Tie the second half of the necklace as a mirror image of the first, ending with 1½" of square knot sinnet. String the wooden bead over all four strands and tie an overhand knot close to the bead. **To clasp:** Slip the bead through the beginning loop.

by Marty Hite

by Marty Hite

Openwork Choker

1mm hemp cord: one 1-yard, one 3½-yard
  length
5 polymer clay crow beads, assorted colors
one 10mm natural wooden bead
basic supplies (see page 1)

1 Center the short strand on the long one, fold in half over a ring and tie an overhand knot ¾" below the ring. Arrange the strands so the two short ends are in the center. Tie a 2" square knot sinnet.

2 Leave a ¾" gap and tie one square knot. Thread a clay bead over the two center strands and push up to the knot.

3 Tie another square knot. Leave a ¾" gap and tie two square knots.

4 Repeat step 2. Leave a ¾" gap and tie two square knots. Thread a clay bead over the two center strands up to the knot. Tie two more square knots. Repeat step 2. Tie a square knot below the bead. Leave a ¾" gap and tie two square knots. Repeat step 2. Tie a square knot below the bead. Leave a ¾" gap. Tie a 2" square knot sinnet. Thread all the ends through the wooden bead, tie in an overhand knot and trim the ends close to the knot. **To clasp:** Slip the bead through the beginning loop.

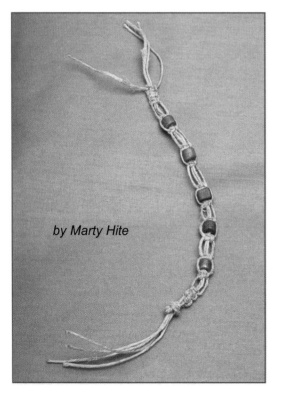
by Marty Hite

Openwork Bracelet

1mm hemp cord: two 12" lengths,
  two 36" lengths
4 polymer clay crow beads, assorted
  colors

one 8mm teal polymer clay cube
  bead
basic supplies (see page 1)

1 Hold all the lengths together, even at one end. Tie an overhand knot, securing the ends to the work ring. Arrange the strands with the 12" lengths in the center. Leave a 2" gap and tie a ⅜" square knot sinnet (3 complete square knots).

2 Leave a ½" gap and tie one square knot. Thread a crow bead over the two center strands up to the knot. Tie another square knot. Repeat four times, placing the cube bead in the center position.

3 Leave a ½" gap and tie a ⅜" square knot sinnet. Tie the ends together in an overhand knot and trim the tails to 2". **To wear:** Wrap the bracelet around your wrist or ankle and tie the tails in a square knot.

Beaded Choker with Filigree

1mm hemp cord: two 24" lengths, two 2½-yard lengths
1 amber glass crow bead or transparent pony bead
ten 8mm black iridescent glass beads
¾" round silver filigree charm
8mm silver jump ring
basic supplies (see page 1)

1 Before beginning, attach the jump ring to the eye of the charm (see page 32). Hold all the strands together and tie an overhand knot in the end. Separate the strands so the long ones are on the outside. Thread all the strands through the amber bead and slide the bead up to the knot. Leave a ½" gap, then tie a 1½" square knot sinnet.

2 Slip a bead over the two center strands and tie a 1" square knot sinnet. Repeat until five beads are strung.

3 Tie three square knots, then slip the jump ring over the lower three strands. Tie three more square knots. Slip a bead over the center two strands and continue working a square knot sinnet, adding a bead every 1", until all the beads are strung.

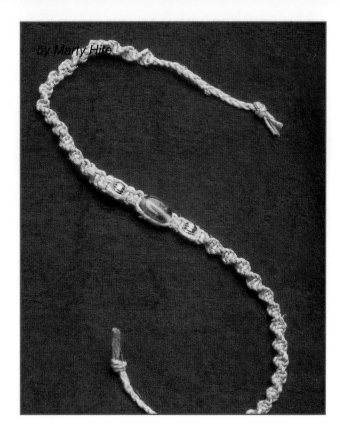

by Marty Hite

4 Tie a 1½" square knot sinnet. Leave a ½" gap, then tie all the strands together in an overhand knot. **To clasp:** Slip the amber bead and knot through the ending gap.

by Marty Hite

Red/Green Fish Necklace

1mm hemp cord: two 3-yard lengths, two 2' lengths
one 1" wide green glass fish bead (lengthwise hole)
four ⅜" wide red glass disk beads
basic supplies (see page 1)

1 Hold all the hemp lengths together and tie an overhand knot close to one end, tighten the knot and secure the knot to a work ring. Braid a four-strand braid for 2", ending with the short strands in the center and the long strands outside.

2 Use the outer strands to tie 6½" of square knot sinnet over the inner strands. Slide two red disk beads over the two center strands and push up to the last knot. Bring the outside strands around the beads and tie three complete square knots over the center strands.

3 Slide the fish bead over the two center strands. Bring the outside strands behind the bead. Tie three complete square knots, pushing the first knot up to the fish. Add the remaining red disks. Bring the outer strands around the beads and tie another 6" of square knot sinnet. Braid 2" of four-strand braid, tie an overhand knot and tighten the knot. Remove from the work ring and trim the hemp close to the knots on each end. **To wear:** Tie the braided ends in a square knot behind your neck.

by Marty Hite
length 9"

Striped Bracelet

20# test hemp cord: one 1½-yard navy blue, one 1½-yard natural length

one 12mm round wooden bead basic supplies (see page 1)

1 Fold the natural strand over the ring so one end extends 12" and the other 36". Tie the blue strand around the natural strand in a half knot, ½" below the ring, making a half knot with one 12" and one 36" tail. Arrange the strands so the short strands are in the center and the blue strands are on the right.

2 Tie an 8" long square knot sinnet. Slide the bead over all the strands, tie an overhand knot and trim the ends to ½". Slip the bracelet off the ring. **To clasp:** Slip the end bead through the beginning loop.

Loop Choker

20# test hemp cord: one 2-yard length, one 6-yard length
one 12mm round wooden bead
basic supplies (see page 1)

1 Fold the 2-yard strand in half over the ring, center the 6-yard strand ¾" from the fold and tie in a half knot.

2 Tie the first half of a square knot. Form the second half, but as you tighten it, leave a ½" loop on the left side. Follow with a full square knot, then create a ½" loop on the right side with the first half of the next square knot. Repeat for 14½".

3 Slide the bead over the strands, tie an overhand knot and trim the ends to 1". Slip the necklace off the ring. **To clasp:** Slip the end bead through the beginning loop.

by Marty Hite
length 17"

by Katie Hacker
length 4½"

Beaded Key Ring

three 24" lengths of 20#
    test hemp cord
wood beads: two
    8mm round, one
    14mmx12mm oval, one
    18mm round carved

one 1" round metal split
    key ring
basic supplies (see
    page 1)

1 Fold the hemp strands in half over the key ring. Tie two square knots with the outer strands over the four center strands. Leave a ¼" gap and tie one square knot; repeat.

2 Slide the oval bead over the drone strands. Tie a square knot and slide an 8mm bead onto each outer strand. Tie a square knot and slide the remaining bead onto the drone strands. Tie an overhand knot and trim the ends to 1½".

Sun/Moon Anklet

red 20# test hemp cord: two 1¾-yard
    lengths, one 18" length
silver beads: two 8mm round rose, one
    16mm sun/moon reversible
basic suplies (see page 1)

1 Hold the strands together, ends even, and tie an overhand knot, leaving 1" tails. Slip the knot into a ring to secure. Braid for 2" and tie an overhand knot. Arrange the strands so the short strand is in the center. Tie a 3" long square knot sinnet. Slide a rose bead onto the drone strand.

2 Tie a 1" long square knot sinnet, then slide the sun/moon bead onto the drone strand. Work another 1" long square knot sinnet, then slide on a rose bead. Tie a 3" long square knot sinnet.

3 Tie all the strands in an overhand knot, then braid for 2". Tie an overhand knot and trim the ends to 1". Slip the anklet off the ring. **To clasp:** Tie the ends in a square knot.

by Katie Hacker
length 16"

Double/Single Square Knot Choker

four 4-yard lengths of 1mm hemp cord
basic supplies (see page 1)

1 Hold all four strands together and fold in half, forming eight strands. Secure the fold to the work ring. Leave a ⅝" gap and tie an overhand knot. Separate the strands, hold the two outer strands together on each side and handle as one to tie a square knot over the four center strands.

2 Divide the strands into two groups of four and begin working alternating square knots, following this pattern: one complete unit, then one unit plus one more complete center square knot. Repeat for 13", or your neck measurement plus 1". End with two side knots.

3 Hold the two outer strands together on each side and handle as one to tie a square knot over the four center strands. Tie all the strands together in an overhand knot and trim the ends close to the knot. **To clasp:** Slip the end knot through the beginning loop.

by Marty Hite

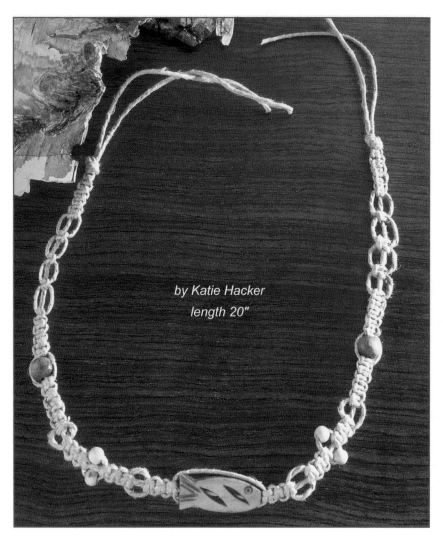

by Katie Hacker
length 20"

Wooden Fish Choker

20# test hemp cord: one 1-yard, two 3-yard
 lengths
wood beads: four 6mm round, two 8mm round,
 one 24mmx10mm fish with a lengthwise hole
basic supplies (see page 1)

1 Hold the strands together, ends even, and tie an overhand knot, leaving 3½" tails. Slip the knot into a ring to secure. Arrange so the short strand is in the center. Tie a ¾" long square knot sinnet. Leave a ¼" gap and tie one square knot; repeat three times for a total of four gaps.

2 Tie a ½" long square knot sinnet, then slide an 8mm bead onto the center strand. Square knot for another ½". Leave a ¼" gap, then tie three square knots. Slide a 6mm bead onto each outer strand, then tie three square knots. Leave a ¼" gap and tie three square knots.

3 Slide the fish onto the center strand. Repeat steps 1-2 in reverse order. Slip the necklace off the ring. **To clasp:** Tie the ends in a square knot.

ALTERNATING SQUARE KNOT:

This technique requires eight strands. To preserve the lacy look, don't pull the knots too tight.
Secure the strands and separate so they lie side by side.

1 Divide into two groups of four. In each group, tie a square knot with the two outer strands over the two center strands.

2 Bring the two left strands of the right group and the two right strands of the left group to the center, dropping the two outer strands on each side.

3 Tie a square knot with the two outer strands over the two center strands. This completes one unit. Repeat step 1 to the desired length.

Around the World Choker & Mushroom Choker

eight 2½-yard strands of 1mm hemp
basic supplies (see page 1)

Around the World choker:
8mm frosted glass beads: 2 blue, 4 green
one ⅜" wide polymer clay millefiori world
  disk bead

Mushroom choker:
3mm polymer clay tube beads: 2 green, 4
  orange
one ⅝" wide blue/white/rainbow polymer
  clay millefiori mushroom bead

Both of these necklaces are made from the same instructions. The bead choice changes the look. The top choker has been worn and shows the softer, smoother look hemp cord acquires in use.

by Marty Hite

1 Hold all eight strands together and tie an overhand knot, securing it to the work ring. Leave a ⅝" gap. Hold the two outer strands together on each side and handle as one to tie a square knot over the four center strands.

2 Divide the strands into two groups of four and begin working alternating square knots. Continue for 5½", ending with the knots on the outside.

3 String a small bead (the color you have fewest of) over the two center strands, bringing three strands down on each side of the bead. Divide the strands into two groups of four and tie one unit of alternating square knots (a square knot on each side, then a center square knot.)

4 On each side of the center knot, string a bead over both strands. Again divide the strands into two groups of four and tie a square knot on each side. String the disk bead on the two center strands. Tie one unit of alternating square knots ending with the center knot. Repeat steps 3-4, ending with the last small bead.

5 Tie alternating square knots for 5½", ending with the knots on the outside. Leave a ⅝" gap and tie all the strands in an overhand knot. **To clasp:** Slip the ending knot through the beginning loop.

13

Wooden Pony Bead Choker

eight 2½-yard strands of 2mm
hemp cord

8 dark brown wooden pony beads
basic supplies (see page 1)

1 Hold all eight strands together and tie an overhand knot, securing it to the work ring. Leave a ¾" gap. Hold the two outer strands together on each side and handle as one to tie a square knot over the four center strands.

2 Tie one unit of alternating square knots, then one more square knot. Repeat four times.

3 Tie the two side knots of another unit, but instead of working a center knot, slide a bead over the two center strands.

4 Make one more unit as in step 2, then repeat step 3. Tie one unit of alternating square knots, then repeat step 3. Tie one unit of alternating square knots, then make another square knot. Slide a bead over both outside strands on each side.

5 Repeat step 3, make one unit of alternating square knots, and repeat step 3. Make a step 2 unit, then repeat step 3. Repeat step 2 (five units), then tie the two side knots of another unit. Bring all the strands together, hold the two outer strands together on each side and handle as one to tie a square knot over the four center strands. Tie an overhand knot and trim the ends. Bring all the strands together, hold the two outer strands together on each side and handle as one to tie a square knot over the four center strands. Tie an overhand knot and trim the ends ½" from the knot. **To clasp:** Slip the end knot through the beginning loop.

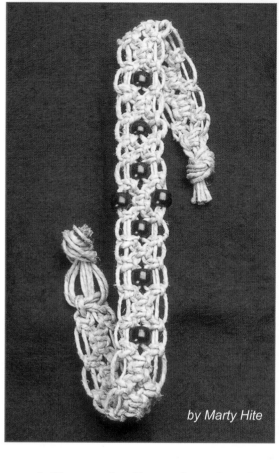

by Marty Hite

by Marty Hite

Interrupted Square Knot Choker

four 4-yard strands of 1mm hemp
ceramic tube beads, assorted colors:

one 14x6mm, ten 8x6mm
basic supplies (see page 1)

1 Hold all the strands together and fold in half; tie an overhand knot 1" from the fold. Hold the two outer strands together on each side and handle as one to tie a square knot over the four center strands.

2 Begin working alternating square knots, but in each unit tie two square knots on each side, then a center knot. Repeat for eight units.

3 Make another step 2 unit, but instead of working a center knot, slide on a small bead. Repeat until all the beads are strung, placing the large bead in the center. Bring all the strands together, hold the two outer strands together on each side and handle as one to tie a square knot over the four center strands. Tie an overhand knot and trim the ends close to the knot. **To clasp:** Slip the end knot through the beginning loop.

Green & Tan Choker

*20# test hemp cord: two 4-yard natural lengths, two 4-yard
      lengths of forest green*
basic supplies (see page 1)

Fold one natural strand in half. Hold the remaining strands
together and tie around the first in a half knot ¾" from the fold.
Slip the knot into a ring to secure. Arrange the strands from left
to right as follows: green, natural, green, natural, natural, green,
natural, green. Tie alternating square knots for 12". Finish the
necklace with an overhand knot. Trim the ends to 1" and slip the
necklace off the ring. **To clasp:** Slip the end knot through the
beginning loop.

Lace Choker

*four 4-yard lengths of 20# test
      hemp*
*beads: two 14mm round carved
      bone, one 16mmx12mm oval
      amber smoked glass*
basic supplies (see page 1)

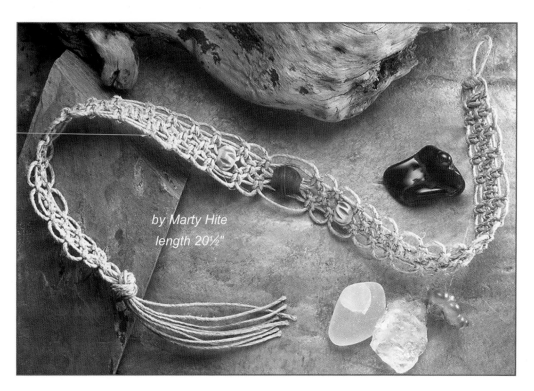

1 Fold one strand in half. Hold the remaining strands together
and tie around the first in a half knot ¾" from the fold. Slip
the knot into a ring to secure. Hold two strands together on each
side and tie a square knot around the other four strands. Tie three
alternating square knot units. Add an additional center knot to the
pattern and continue for 5½" stopping at a set of right and left knots.

2 Add a bone bead to the two center strands. Tie an alternating
square knot unit, then another right and left. Slip the glass bead
onto the four center strands. Repeats steps 1-2 in reverse order, but
after the last square knot tie an overhand knot and trim the ends
to 3¼". Slip the necklace off the ring. **To clasp:** Slip the end knot
through the beginning loop.

by Marty Hite

Lacy Beaded Choker

four 4-yard lengths of 1mm hemp cord
fifteen 7x12mm dark brown wooden beads
basic supplies (see page 1)

1 Hold all four strands together and fold in half, forming eight strands. Secure the fold to the work ring. Leave a ⅝" gap. Hold the two outer strands together on each side and handle as one to tie a square knot over the four center strands. Divide the strands into two groups of four.

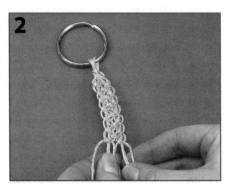

2 Tie alternating square knots for 2", ending with the knots on the outside.

3 Slide a bead over the two center strands. Tie alternating square knots for five more square knots–two outside, one center, two outside.

4 Thread the two center strands through a bead from opposite directions as shown. Tie five more alternating square knots. Repeat steps 3 and 4 until all the beads are strung. Tie alternating square knots for 2". Hold the two outer strands together on each side and tie one square knot over the four center strands. Leave a ½" gap and tie all the strands in an overhand knot. **To clasp:** Slip the end knot through the beginning loop.

Buttonhole Choker

four 4-yard strands of 1mm hemp
basic supplies (see page 1)

by Marty Hite

1 Hold all the strands together and fold in half; tie an overhand knot ½" from the fold. Hold the two outer strands together on each side and handle as one to tie a square knot over the four center strands.

2 Tie alternating square knots for six complete units, then tie two complete side knots. Drop the two outer strands on each side and use the center four strands to tie a ½" square knot sinnet.

3 Tie alternating square knots for three units. Divide the strands into two groups of four. With each group, tie a ½" square knot sinnet. Drop the two outer strands on each side and begin working by alternating square knot with a center knot; tie three units, ending with the side knots. Drop the two outer strands on each side and use the center four strands to tie a ½" square knot sinnet.

4 Repeat step 3 twice. Tie alternating square knots for six complete units–for the last center knot of the last unit, hold the two outer strands on each side together and handle as one to make a square knot over the center strands. Tie all the strands in an overhand knot. **To clasp:** Slip the end knot through the beginning loop. Add a bead if desired.

Plain but Pretty Choker

1mm hemp cord: one 48" length, two 5-yard lengths
one 10mm round wooden bead
basic supplies (see page 1)

1 Hold all the strands together and fold in half; tie an overhand knot ⅝" from the fold. Arrange the strands with the two short ends in the center.

by Marty Hite

2 Drop the two outer strands and tie a square knot sinnet with the remaining strands for three complete square knots.

3 Pick up the dropped strands. Handle the two outer strands on each side as one to tie a square knot sinnet for three complete square knots.

4 Repeat steps 2-3 to the desired length. Slide the bead over all six ends and snug it close to the last square knot. Tie an overhand knot close to the knot. **To clasp:** Slip the bead through the beginning loop.

HALF KNOT SINNET:

Also called a half knot spiral, this knot gives the effect of a flat twisted ribbon. It is worked just like a square knot sinnet, but with half knots.

Make a half knot, with the left strand passing in front of the drone strands and the right passing behind, so the drone strands are enclosed in a loop. Repeat. The knots will form a spiral as the sinnet grows.

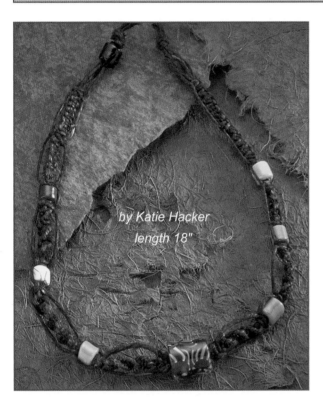

by Katie Hacker
length 18"

Yin Yang Bracelet

Millefiori Necklace

black 20# test hemp cord: one 24", two 36", two 54" lengths
glass tube beads: 7 assorted 8mm, one 18mmx14mm millefiori
basic supplies (see page 1)

1 Hold the strands together, ends even, and tie an overhand knot, leaving ½" tails. Slip the knot into a ring to secure. Leave a ¾" gap.

2 Tie the 36" strands over the others in a square knot. Drop the 36" strands and square knot the 54" strands over the 24" strands for 1". Repeat once.

3 Tie the 36" strands over the other strands in a square knot. Slide an 8mm bead onto the 24" and 54" strands. Tie the 36" strands over the others in a square knot. Drop the 36" strands. Use the 54" strands to tie a 1" long half knot sinnet over the 24" strands. Repeat twice. Tie the 36" strands over the other strands in a square knot.

4 Slide the 18mm bead over all the strands. Repeat steps 2-3 in reverse order. Leave a ¾" gap, then slide an 8mm bead over the strands, tie an overhand knot and trim the ends to ½". Slip the necklace off the ring. **To clasp:** Slip the end bead through the beginning loop.

blue 20# test hemp cord: one 28", two 1¼-yard lengths
beads: two 6mm frosted white glass tubes, two 8mm silver fluted
  round, one 24mm blue/red cloisonné disk with yin yang symbol
basic supplies (see page 1)

1 Hold the strands together, ends even, and tie an overhand knot, leaving 2½" tails. Slip the knot into a ring to secure. Arrange the strands with the short one in the center. Tie a 2½" long half knot sinnet. Tie a square knot, then slide a white bead onto the drone strands.

2 Tie two square knots, then slide a silver bead onto the drone strands. Tie four square knots, then slide the yin yang bead onto the drone strand. Repeat steps 1 and 2 in reverse order. Slip the bracelet off the ring. **To clasp:** Tie the ends in a square knot.

by Katie Hacker
length 18"

Purple Spiral Anklet

20# test hemp cord: one 1-yard purple, one 14" purple, one 1-yard natural, one 14" natural length
basic supplies (see page 1)

Hold the strands together, ends even, and tie an overhand knot, leaving 2½" tails. Slip the knot into a ring to secure. Arrange the strands with the short strands in the center. Tie a 9" long half knot sinnet. Tie an overhand knot and trim the ends to 2½". Slip the anklet off the ring. **To clasp:** Tie the ends in a square knot.

by Marty Hite
length 14"

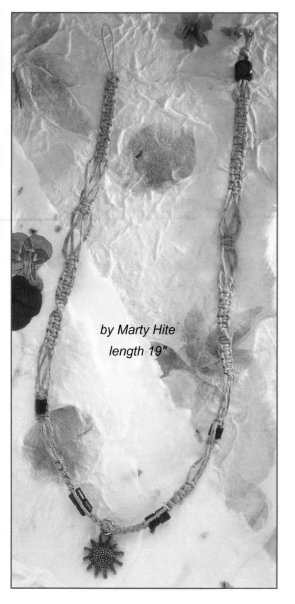

by Marty Hite
length 19"

Crossover Sunflower Necklace

20# test hemp cord: one 1-yard, one 5-yard length
beads: four 8mm red ceramic tubes, two 8mm brown ceramic tubes, one 12mm square wooden
one 2mm pewter sunflower charm with jump ring
basic supplies (see page 1)

1 Fold the 1-yard strand in half over a ring, center the remaining strand ¾" from the fold and tie a half knot. Arrange the strands with the short ones in the center.

2 Tie a 1½" long square knot sinnet. Bring the center strands over the outer strands to the outside (one crossover). Tie two square knots with the new outside strands ¾" below the last square knot.

3 Make another crossover and tie a ¾" long square knot sinnet. Tie a ¼" long half knot sinnet (or one full twist). Tie a ½" long square knot sinnet. Make a crossover and tie a square knot. Slide a red bead over the two center strands. Tie a square knot and make a crossover. Tie a ½" long square knot sinnet. Slide a brown and red bead over the center strands. Tie a ½" long square knot sinnet and thread the left strand through the jump ring of the charm.

4 Repeat steps 2-3 in reverse order. Slide the wood bead over the strands, tie an overhand knot and trim the ends to ½". Slip the necklace off the ring. **To clasp:** Slip the end bead through the beginning loop.

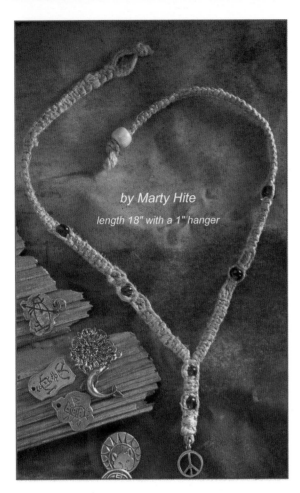

Peace Y-Necklace

20# test hemp cord: two 1-yard, two 4-yard lengths
round beads: six 8mm blue glass, one 12mm wood

one 14mm flat pewter peace charm with jump ring
basic supplies (see page 1)

1 Hold the 1-yard strands together, ends even, and fold them in half through the charm jump ring. Hold the 4-yard strands together and tie in a half knot around the other strands, below the jump ring. Slip the knot into a ring to secure. Arrange the strands so the short strands are in the center. Square knot the longer strands around them three times. Slide a blue bead onto the drone strands. Tie three square knots and add another bead. Tie one square knot.

2 Divide the strands into two sections, with two long and two short strands in each. **For each:** Use the long strands to tie a 1¼" long square knot sinnet. Leave a ¼" gap, tie one square knot, then string a blue bead over the drone strands. Tie a square knot, then leave a ¼" gap. Tie a 1" long square knot sinnet. Slide a bead over the drone strands. Tie a 4½" long square knot sinnet.

3 On one side, slide the wooden bead over all the strands and tie an overhand knot. On the other side, leave a ¾" gap and tie an overhand knot. Trim all ends to ¼". Slip the necklace off the ring. **To clasp:** Slip the end bead through the end loop.

by Marty Hite
length 18" with a 1" hanger

Green Center Bead Bracelet

1mm hemp cord: one 18", two 36" strands
one 9x15mm green glass bicone oval bead
two 8mm round brass melon beads
basic supplies (see page 1)

Follow the instructions for the Purple Center Bead Bracelet on page 5. Substitute a half knot sinnet for a square knot sinnet. In steps 2 and 3, substitute the beads listed above.

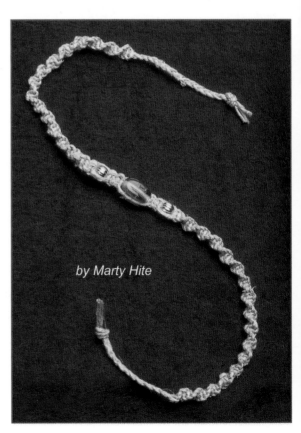

by Marty Hite

HALF KNOT SPIRAL:

Also called a half-knot sinnet, this gives the effect of a flat, twisted ribbon. It is worked just like a square knot sinnet, but with half knots.

1 Make a half knot, with the left strand passing in front of the drone strands and the right passing behind, so that the drone strands are enclosed in a loop.

2 Repeat step 1. The knots will form a spiral as the sinnet grows.

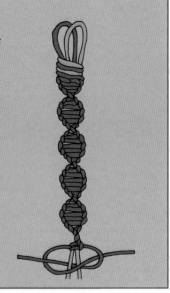

Spiral Sunflower Necklace

1mm hemp cord: two 24",
two 2½-yard lengths
three 8mm round brass
beads
polymer clay sunflower tube
beads: one 6x14mm, two
6x18mm
basic supplies (see page 1)

by Marty Hite

1 Hold all the strands together and tie an overhand knot near one end. Thread a brass bead over all four strands up to the knot. Arrange the strands so the longer lengths are on the outside and tie a square knot ½" below the bead.

2 Tie a half-knot sinnet for 6".

3 Thread a 6x18mm bead over the two center strands, then tie five more half-knots. Repeat with a brass bead, the 6x14mm bead, and another brass bead. String the last bead and tie a half-knot sinnet for 6".

4 Tie a square knot, leave a ½"-⅝" gap, and tie an overhand knot. **To clasp:** Slip the beginning bead through the end loop. The fit should be snug.

HALF-HITCH SPIRAL:

This spiral gives the effect of a corkscrew–one cord wrapped spiral-fashion around a straight cord.

A **half hitch** is simply a single wrap of one stranad around another, in which the tail of the first strand is brought over itself between the two strands, then down. Use one strand to tie a series of half hitches around the other strand. The knots form a spiral.

Buffalo Charm Pendant

1mm hemp cord: one 18"- 24", one 4'-5' length
two ⅜" long red glass nugget beads
one 1" wide silver jump ring
one 6mm silver jump ring
basic supplies (see page 1)

by Marty Hite

Before beginning, attach the charm to the jump ring (see page 32).

1 Hold all the strands together and tie an overhand knot near one end. Leave a 2" gap and tie another overhand knot.

2 Use the longer length to knot a half-hitch around the shorter length. Continue to tie a half-hitch spiral for 7".

3 Thread a red bead over the center strand, then tie 1" more of half-hitch spiral. Slip the jump ring over the spiral.

4 Thread a red bead over the center strand, then tie 7" more of half-hitch spiral. Tie an overhand knot, leave a 2" gap and tie another overhand knot. **To wear:** Tie the knotted ends together behind your neck.

HALF-HITCH:

Half-hitch is a single warp of one strand around another. Bring the end between the working and drone strands.

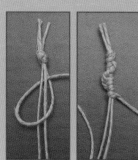

Half hitch spiral: This sinnet gives a corkscrew effect. Use one strand to tie a series of half-hitches around the other strand–the knots will form a spiral.

Alternating half-hitch: This variation of the half-hitch provides a flat sinnet rather than a spiral. Half-hitch the left strand around the center strand, then half-hitch the right strand around the center strand. Flatten the knots with your fingers.

Zipper Bracelet

20# test hemp cord: one 1-yard natural length, one 14" natural length, one 1-yard purple length, one 14" purple length
basic supplies (see page 1)

Hold the strands together, ends even, and tie an overhand knot, leaving 2½" tails. Slip the knot into a ring to secure. Arrange the strands so the short strands are in the center. Tie alternating half hitches for 9". Finish the bracelet with an overhand knot. Trim the ends to 2½". Slip the bracelet off the ring. **To clasp:** Tie the ends in a square knot.

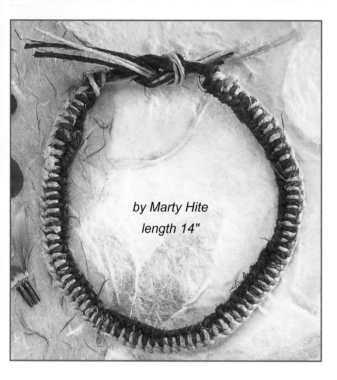

by Marty Hite
length 14"

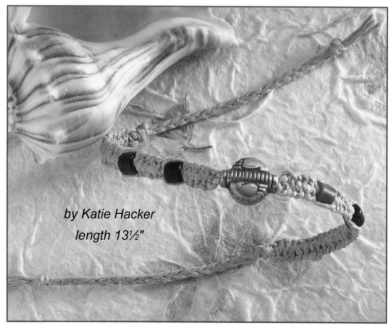

by Katie Hacker
length 13½"

Beaded Anklet

20# test hemp cord: one 1-yard, two 1¾-yard lengths
beads: 4 assorted 8mm frosted glass tubes, one 16mm wide silver disk
basic supplies (see page 1)

1 Hold the strands together, ends even, and tie an overhand knot, leaving 1" tails. Slip the knot into a ring to secure. Braid for 2½", then tie an overhand knot.

2 Arrange the strands so the short strand is in the center. Tie alternating half-hitch knots for 1½". Slide a tube bead onto the drone strand, tie alternating half-hitch knots for ½" and repeat. Slide the silver bead over all the strands, then repeat steps 1 and 2 in reverse order. Slip the anklet off the ring. **To clasp:** Tie the ends in a square knot.

Tri-Color Anklet

1⅓-yard lengths of 20# test hemp cord: 1 green, 1 red, 1 blue

8mm round frosted glass beads: 1 green, 1 red, 1 blue

basic supplies (see page 1)

Hold the strands together and tie an overhand knot, leaving 3½" tails. Slip the knot into a ring to secure. Tie the red strand in a half-hitch spiral around the other strands for 3". Use the blue to tie a half-hitch spiral for 1½", then slide the red, blue and green beads over all the strands. Continue the half-hitch with the blue hemp for 1½". Tie the green in a half-hitch for 3", then finish the anklet with an overhand knot. Trim the ends to 3½" and slip the anklet off the ring. **To clasp:** Tie the ends in a square knot.

by Katie Hacker
length 17"

by Katie Hacker
length 19"

Protective Hand Necklace

20# test hemp cord: one 2-yard, one 6-yard length

one 12mm round wood bead

one 22mm long gold protective hand charm

one 8mm gold jump ring

basic supplies (see page 1)

1 Fold both strands in half over a ring and tie an overhand knot 1" below the fold. Arrange the strands with the shorter ones in the center and tie a 3" long half knot sinnet. Drop the outer strands and knot one center strand around the other to make a 1" long half-hitch spiral. Repeat the half knot/half-hitch sequence three times.

2 Tie a half knot spiral for 3". Slide the wood bead over all the strands, then tie an overhand knot. Trim the ends to ¼" and slip the necklace off the ring. Attach the charm to a jump ring, then attach the jump ring (see page 32) to the necklace center. **To clasp:** Slip the end bead through the beginning loop.

ALTERNATING HALF-HITCH:

A half-hitch is simply a single wrap of one strand around another, in which the tail of the first strand is brought over itself between the two strands, then down.

1 Tying with two strands, half-hitch the left strand around the right strand, then half-hitch the right strand around the left strand. Continue to the desired length.

2 To make a **half-hitch sinnet**, tie each half-hitch around the opposite working strand and all the drone strands.

Five-Bead Choker

2mm hemp cord: one 5-yard, one 1-yard strand
5 glass crow beads: 2 silver, 3 varied colors
basic supplies (see page 1)

1 Center the short strand on the long strand, fold in half over a ring and tie an overhand knot ¾" below the ring. Arrange the strands so the two shorter ends are in the center. Tie an alternating half-hitch for 5".

2 String a silver bead over the center two strands. Bring the long strand around the outside of the bead and tie an alternating half-hitch for ¾".

by Marty Hite

3 Repeat step 2 with each of the colored beads. String a silver bead and continue an alternating half-hitch for 5". Tie an overhand knot and trim excess cord. **To clasp:** Slip the end knot through the beginning loop.

by Marty Hite

Toadstool Bracelet

1mm hemp cord: two 36" strands, two 12"
*   strands*
two 8mm black iridescent glass beads
one ⅜" wide polymer clay millefiori toadstool
*   bead*
basic supplies (see page 1)

1 Hold the strands together, ends even, and tie onto a ring with an overhand knot, leaving 2½" tails. Arrange the strands so the shorter strands are in the center. Tie an alternating half-hitch for 2½".

2 String a bead over the two center strands. Bring the long strands around the outside of the bead and tie six more alternating half-hitches.

3 Repeat step 2 with the toadstool bead, then string the second glass bead and continue to tie an alternating half-hitch for 2½". Tie an overhand knot and trim the tails to 2½". Cut the bracelet off the work ring, leaving 2½" tails. **To wear:** Wrap the bracelet around your wrist or ankle and tie the tails in an overhand knot, leaving a tassel.

VERTICAL LARK'S HEAD CHAIN:

Bulkier than many other knots, the vertical lark's head is a spectacular knot when coupled with hanging ornaments.

1 Loop the working strand or strands (either the right or left) around the front of the drones, bringing the ends between the strands.

2 Bring the working strands behind the drones below the first loop. Bring the end over the drone and through the new loop; tighten.

by Katie Hacker
length 17"

Fish & Bell Necklace

20# test hemp cord: two 3½-yard lengths, two 1½-yard lengths
beads: two 18mm silver fleur-de-lis, one 12mm black glass tube
charms: four 8mm silver temple bells, one 28mm silver fish
one 8mm siler jump ring
basic supplies (see page 1)

1 Hold the strands together, ends even, with the longer strands on the left, and tie an overhand knot, leaving ½" tails. Slip the knot into a ring to secure. Leave a ¾" gap, then hold the left strands together and tie a vertical lark's head knot around the shorter right strands. Continue knotting for 4½".

2 Slide an 18mm bead onto the right strands and up to the last knot. Leave the left strands in a pronounced loop. Tie lark's head knots for ¾". Slide two bells onto the left strands up to the last knot. Continue knotting for ¾". Leave a ½" loop, then knot for another ¾".

3 Slide two bells onto the left strands, up to the last knot. Knot for another ¾". Slide the 18mm bead onto the drone strands, then continue knotting for 4¹/₂".

2 Slide the black bead over all the strands, then tie an overhand knot and trim the ends to ½". Slip the necklace off the ring. Attach the fish to the jump ring (see page 32), then attach the jump ring to the center loop as shown. **To clasp:** Slip the end bead through the beginning loop.

ALTERNATING LARK'S HEAD CHAIN:

A more decorative version of the vertical lark's head, the alternating lark's head allows the designer more freedom to use loops for decoration.

Starting either on the left or right, make a vertical lark's head knot with the outermost strand around the drones. Drop that strand and pick up the opposite outer strand to make another knot. Continue, alternating sides.

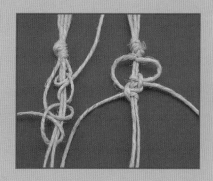

Forest Choker

20# test forest green hemp cord: two 2-yard, two 22" lengths
four 8mm round wood beads
basic supplies (see page 1)

1 Hold the long strands together, ends even, then place the short strands over the longer strands 6" from the ends. Tie an overhand knot. Slip the knot into a ring to secure. Tie the longer strands around the short ones in alternating lark's head knots for 5".

2 Slide a bead onto the center strands up to the last knot, then tie two alternating lark's head knots, one on each side; repeat three times. Tie alternating lark's head knots for another 5", then finish the necklace with an overhand knot. Trim the ends to 6", trim the short strands close to the knot and slip the necklace off the ring. **To clasp:** Tie the ends in a square knot.

by Katie Hacker
length 24"

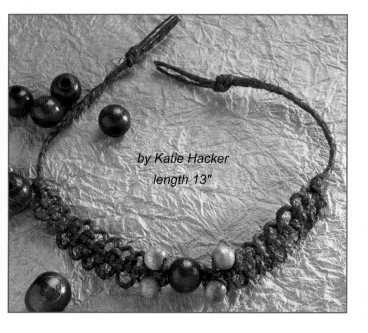

by Katie Hacker
length 13"

Purple & Wood Bracelet

20# test purple hemp cord: one 1-yard, two 1¾-yard lengths
round wood beads: four 8mm, one 12mm
basic supplies (see page 1)

1 Hold the strands together, ends even, and tie an overhand knot, leaving 1" tails. Slip the knot into a ring to secure. Braid for 2½", then tie another overhand knot. Tie the longer strands around the shorter strand in alternating lark's head knots for 2".

2 Slide a bead onto each working strand and tie each strand in a lark's head knot around the center strand. Slide the large bead over all the strands, then repeat steps 1 and 2 in reverse order to finish the bracelet. Slip the bracelet off the ring. **To clasp:** Tie the ends in a square knot.

CHINESE CROWN KNOT:

The Chinese crown knot is an interesting knot that, when done properly, looks like a box on one side and a cross on the other.

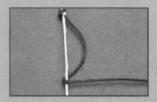

1 Wrap the right strand under and around the left cord in an R-shape.

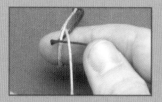

2 Wrap the strand now on the left behind, up and through the top and fold it down over the front.

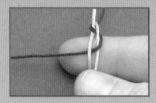

3 Tuck the right strand across the front and through the lower left loop.

4 Tighten each strand individually, adjusting to prevent uneven gaps above the knot.

by Katie Hacker
length 20"

Celestial Necklace

six 1-yard lengths of 20# test hemp cord
one 30mm sun/moon silver charm
basic supplies (see page 1)

1 Divide the hemp into two groups of three strands. Braid each group. Hold the groups together, ends even and tie in an overhand knot, leaving 1" tails. Leave a 2" gap, then tie them together in a Chinese crown knot. Repeat twice, adjusting the braids as you tie the Chinese crown to make the gaps 2" wide.

2 Slide the charm onto the upper braid and tie the Chinese crown, making sure the charm is facing the front. Leave a 2" gap and tie a Chinese crown again. Repeat twice, then leave a 2" gap and tie the ends in a overhand knot. Trim the ends to 1" and slip the necklace off the ring. **To clasp:** Slip the beginning knot through the end loop.

JOSEPHINE KNOT:

The Josephine knot is an elegant knot that looks best in long, lacy designs with many strands. It is very easy and distinctive.

1 Make a loop with the left strands as shown.

2 Place the right strands over this loop, then slide the right strands behind the left loose strand ends.

3 Slide the strand ends over the top left strands and weave the strand diagonally across the loop. Tighten the knot evenly.

by Katie Hacker
length 15½"

Josephine Knot Choker

three 3-yard lengths of 20# test forest green hemp cord
one 12mm round wood bead
basic supplies (see page 1)

1 Hold the strands together, ends even, and fold in half over a ring. Leave a ¾" gap and tie an overhand knot. Tie a Josephine knot 1" from the overhand knot.

2 Leave a 1" space and tie a Josephine knot. Repeat until 2½" from the end of the strands.

3 Leave a 1" space from the last knot and tie an overhand knot. Slide the bead onto the strands, then finish the choker with an overhand knot. Trim the ends to ¼" and slip the necklace off the ring. **To clasp:** Slip the end bead through the beginning loop.

Josephine Knot Anklet

20# test blue hemp cord: four
2-yard lengths, two 1-yard
lengths
silver beads: one 14mmx10mm
oval, two 6mm tube
basic supplies (see page 1)

by Katie Hacker
length 15"

1 Hold the strands together, ends even, and tie an overhand knot, leaving ¼" tails. Slip the knot into a ring to secure. Divide the strands into three groups of two and braid for 2½".

2 Tie the 2-yard lengths over the shorter lengths in a square knot. Leave a ½" gap, then tie a Josephine knot, leaving the shorter strands free. Leave a ½" gap and gather all the strands into an overhand knot. Repeat. Repeat again; but tie an overhand knot in the loose strands, slide a tube bead onto these strands and overhand knot to secure. The bead should show in the 1" gap.

3 Repeat again, but tie the center strands in an overhand knot, slide the 16mm bead onto the center strands and tie an overhand knot to secure. The bead should show in the 1" gap. Tie an overhand knot in the loose strands, slide a tube bead onto these strands and overhand knot to secure. The bead should show in the 1" gap. Repeat step 1 in reverse order and slip the anklet off the ring. **To clasp:** Tie the braids in a square knot.

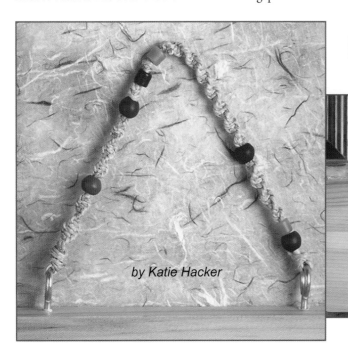

by Katie Hacker

Hemp Hanger for Frame

Sand and seal the frame and insert eye screws 4" apart in the middle. Align three hemp strands and tie in an overhand knot around one eye screw. Tie half knots (see page 18), inserting beads evenly spaced along the strand. Finish by knotting in an overhand knot around the other eye screw. Insert the picture and glue a piece of decorative paper to the front of the frame. Write a name on white paper and glue it to the decorative paper.

They say everything old is new again, and so it seems with the 1960s and '70s crafts' return. Today, you'll find the tie-dyed shirts, candle making and here comes macramé! These easy to make natural-looking jewelry pieces are the newest version of macramé. You can make necklaces, bracelets, anklets or anything you like. It's fast, easy and uniquely your own. Enjoy!

Adding Length to Hemp Strands:

If you run out of hemp before the end of a project, or simply wish to make the project longer, tie an extra strand onto each strand of the project using an overhand knot to give yourself the extra length. No one will be able to see where these "new" strands begin. Some of the projects in this book use this technique and it is impossible to tell which ones!

Modifying a Project:

You may wish to modify a jewelry piece to make it either longer or shorter than the designer's—depending on where you wish to put it. A simple way to determine how long the piece needs to be is to measure where you want to put it (wrist, neck, etc.) and add two inches. This is how long your piece needs to be, including the clasp.

The simplest way to modify a project is to add to or subtract length from the clasps. For plain end clasps, leave a few extra inches of ends to make sure you have room to tie on your piece. For other types of clasps, a little more planning is needed, but it is still a relatively simple process. Just remember to keep your jewelry symmetrical by adjusting the length on both sides of the piece.

Mix & Match Clasps:

Hemp softens as it is worn, acquiring a comfortable, cottony feel. The surface fibers interlock to produce a smoother appearance, and the knots become nearly impossible to undo. If, like many people, you will wear your jewelry day-in and day-out, you don't need a clasp—just tie the ends together. If, however, you would like to be able to remove it without cutting it off, either make a clasp or braid each end for 2" (braided strands make a larger knot which is easier to untie).

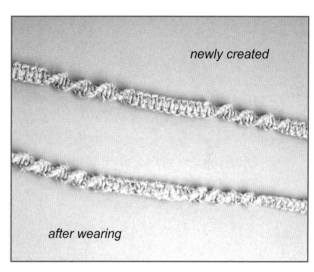

newly created

after wearing

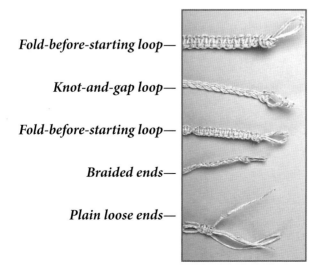

Fold-before-starting loop—

Knot-and-gap loop—

Fold-before-starting loop—

Braided ends—

Plain loose ends—

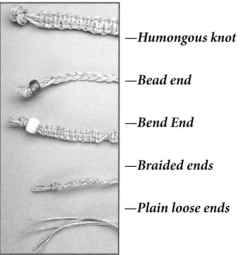

—*Humongous knot*

—*Bead end*

—*Bend End*

—*Braided ends*

—*Plain loose ends*

Getting Started:

In order to maintain even tension as you work, it's necessary to secure the cord ends. Cut your strands then align the ends together and (usually, make an overhand knot. Slip the knot into the slot of the split ring, or hook it onto a curtain ring. Hook the ring on a stable object such as a clothes hook or doorknob (the designers have been known to use their big toes, which are wonderfully portable). Some projects call for strands to be cut twice as long, then folded in half. In those cases, just loop the fold over the ring. Remove the project from the ring before tightening the knots.

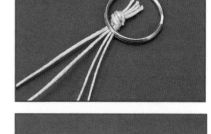

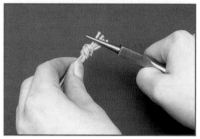

Tightening: The beginning and ending knots of a project should be tightened with pliers to secure them. Grasp each strand, one at a time, in the pliers and pull it firmly away from the knot.

Vocabulary:

Throughout the book words will be used that may need an explanation—
Drone: This is a strand in the design that does not "work"; other strands are knotted around it. These strands are important as they are often the ones beads are placed on and the ones that add bulk to the project.
Sinnet: A series of knots of the same type forming a pattern.
Working Strand: These are the strands you knot with, usually the longest strands of the design.

How to Attach a Jump Ring:

It helps to have two pairs of pliers or tweezers. To open the ring, grasp the jump ring on each side of the opening and move them in opposite directions like opening a door. Don't pull the ends away from each other (like opening a book), as that will distort the shape of the ring and you will find it impossible to get the ends to meet properly when you reclose it. Hook the ring through the eye or loop and rotate the ends back to their original position. Turn the ring so the opening is at the back.

right

About the Designers:

Katie Hacker started making jewelry as a teenager because she couldn't find cool clip earrings for her un-pierced ears. Now, Katie hosts the public television series *Beads, Baubles & Jewels*, writes instructional books, contributes to magazines and teaches workshops. Katie specializes in showing beginning beaders how easy it is to create stylish, boutique-style jewelry. And she finally got her ears pierced! Read Katie's Beading Blog at **www.KatieHacker.com**.

Marty Hite has always loved beading and jewelry making. So, naturally, when hemp jewelry became popular among her friends she set out to learn how to make her own. Finding little information available in print, she taught herself out of old macramé books and by trial and error. This is her second book.